Our Civic Life
Democracy and Decision Making

by Lisa Moran

Table of Contents

Millmark
EDUCATION

In the United States (U.S.), we elect a president every four years. People decide which **candidate** will get their vote. During the presidential **campaign**, the candidates work hard to win votes.

In 1860, Abraham Lincoln and three other candidates were running for president. Look at the images from the presidential **election** of 1860. Discuss the images with questions like these.

What details do you notice in the illustration of Lincoln's return to Springfield?

What is the cartoon saying about Abraham Lincoln and the other candidates?

What are some ways that elections have changed since 1860.

candidate – a person who tries to be elected or chosen for a position

campaign – the actions taken before an election to win votes

election – the act of choosing leaders by voting

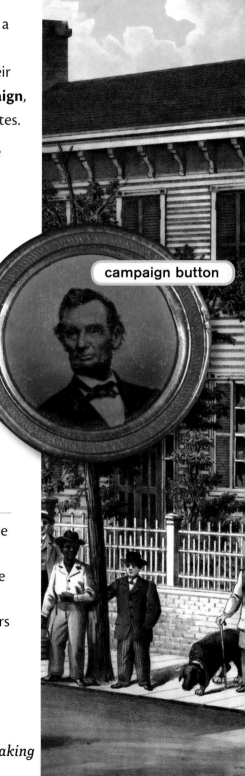

campaign button

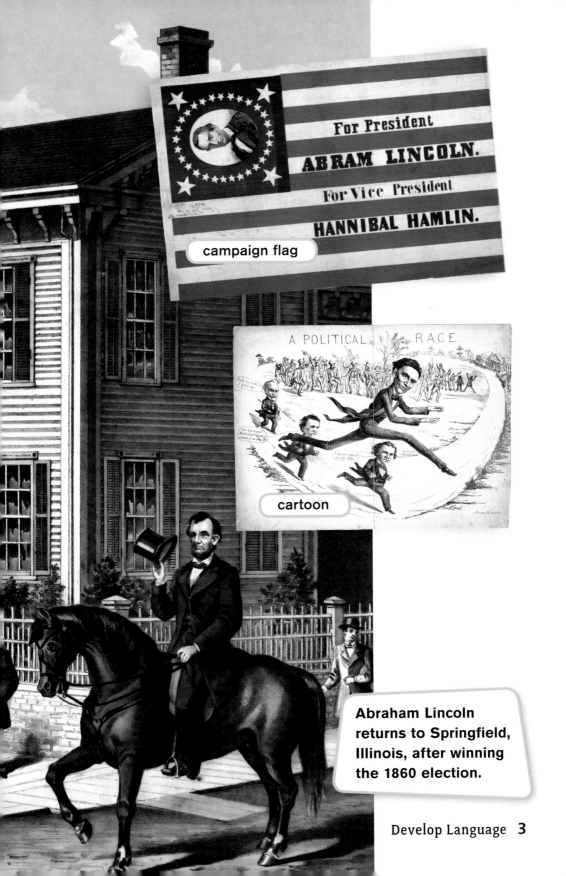

campaign flag

For President
ABRAM LINCOLN.
For Vice President
HANNIBAL HAMLIN.

A POLITICAL RACE.

cartoon

Abraham Lincoln returns to Springfield, Illinois, after winning the 1860 election.

CHAPTER 1

Our Rights and Responsibilities

The United States is a **democracy**. In a democracy, people elect their leaders. The leaders serve in the **government**. In a democracy, people have certain **rights**, or freedoms. The government protects the rights of the people.

Our democracy in the United States is based on the **Constitution**, a document that describes the organization of the U.S. government. The **Bill of Rights** is part of the Constitution. It protects the rights of people in the United States.

U.S. Constitution

democracy – a form of government in which people elect their leaders

government – a system through which some people rule others

rights – guarantees of freedoms

Constitution – the document that tells how the U.S. government works

Bill of Rights – the part of the Constitution that lists some of our rights

KEY IDEA In a democracy, people elect their government leaders.

The Bill of Rights was added to the Constitution as a list of ten **amendments**, or additions, in 1791. Some of these amendments are described in the chart below.

amendments – changes or additions to a document

Amendment	What It Means
1st Amendment: Freedom of religion, speech, press, assembly, and petition	The government must allow people to: • practice any religion they choose; • say what they think in public; • have news that is not controlled by the government; • gather with others in groups; • disagree with the government.
4th Amendment: Protection from unreasonable search and seizure	The government cannot search a home or take someone's possessions unless: • it gets permission from a court, and, • it gives the court an acceptable reason for the search.
5th Amendment: Protection from double jeopardy and self-incrimination	People cannot be tried twice in court for the same crime. People do not have to testify in court against themselves.
6th Amendment: The right to a speedy, public trial by jury, and the right to counsel	If a person is accused of a crime, the person has the right to have: • a trial, without delay, that is public, not secret; • a jury that decides if the person is innocent or guilty; • a lawyer who will represent the person in court.

Responsibilities of People and the Government

People who live in a democracy have **responsibilities**, as well as rights. In the United States, everyone is responsible for obeying the laws and respecting the rights of others. Everyone is responsible for paying taxes.

In a democracy, the government has responsibilities, too. The United States has local, state, and federal governments. Each of these three levels of government has certain responsibilities.

responsibilities – what a person must do, or should do

▲ **People line up at the post office to mail their tax forms.**

Levels of Government
Local
• the government of a town, city, or county
• located in a community
State
• the government of each state
• located in the capital of each state
Federal
• the national government
• located in Washington D.C.

◀ **Colorado's state government is located in Denver, the capital.**

Each level of government protects people and provides **services** that help them. The money from taxes and other sources helps pay for these services.

Counties, cities, and other areas where people live have local governments.

Every state has its own government, located in the capital of the state. For example, the government of Colorado is located in Denver, the capital.

The federal government is our national government. It is located in Washington, D.C. The president, the Congress, and the Supreme Court are all part of the federal government.

services – tasks, or work, that a government does to help people

Some Government Responsibilities

Level of Government	Examples
Local Responsibilities • police • fire protection	
State Responsibilities • education • road construction	
Federal Responsibilities • postal service • military protection	

KEY IDEAS In the United States, people have certain rights and responsibilities. In the U.S., governments protect people and provide services.

The Rights and Responsibilities of Citizens

Everyone in the United States has rights and responsibilities. **Citizens** have additional rights and responsibilities.

A citizen is a member of a nation. Every nation has its own laws about **citizenship**, or being a citizen. In the United States, you are a citizen if you were born in the United States, or if your parents are U.S. citizens. You can also become a U.S. citizen by passing a test.

Only U.S. citizens can be elected to **public office**. Only U.S. citizens can vote in elections or serve on juries. For U.S. citizens, voting and serving on a jury are both rights and responsibilities.

citizens – members of a nation
citizenship – being a citizen
public office – a position in a government

▲ **Citizens vote to elect their leaders.**

▲ **Citizens can serve on juries. A jury listens to all the facts before deciding if a law was broken.**

KEY IDEA Citizens have additional rights and responsibilities.

INFER

Explain what these people are doing.

Infer if this kind of activity is protected by the Bill of Rights.

MAKE CONNECTIONS

Think about your community. Where is your local government located? Who are the leaders of your local government? When were those leaders elected? Create a fact sheet about your local government.

USE THE LANGUAGE OF SOCIAL STUDIES

What is freedom of assembly?

Freedom of assembly is the right to gather in groups and hold meetings.

CHAPTER 2

Practicing Democratic Ideals

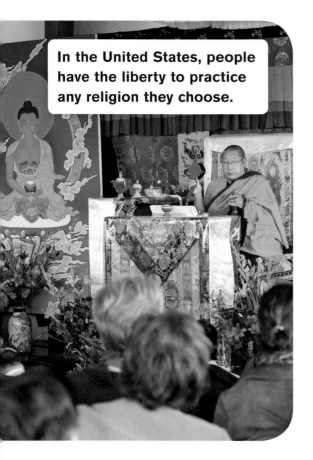

In the United States, people have the liberty to practice any religion they choose.

Over time, people have developed certain beliefs about how to live in a democracy. These beliefs are called **democratic ideals**.

Equality is a democratic ideal. This is the belief that all people should have the same rights under the law. For example, U.S. laws say that you cannot refuse to sell a home to someone because of the person's race, sex, or religion.

Liberty is another democratic ideal. Liberty is the belief that people should live in the way they choose, as long as they respect the liberty of others and obey the law.

democratic ideals – beliefs about what is best or most important in a democracy

equality – when all people have the same rights under the law

liberty – freedom to live the way we choose

Another important democratic ideal is called the **common good**. The common good is what is best for the people in a local, state, or national community, such as being healthy and safe.

There are different ways to work for the common good. Police officers and firefighters work for the common good by keeping people safe. **Volunteers** work for the common good by giving their time to help others. Sometimes people give money, clothing, or other items to organizations that help people.

▶ **People can contribute to the common good by volunteering to help others.**

Another way to work for the common good is to participate in government. People can volunteer to work for a candidate or a cause, such as protecting the environment. People can also become candidates themselves.

common good – what is best for the people in a local, state, or national community

volunteers – people who work without being paid

Bʏ Tʜᴇ Wᴀʏ...

César Chávez (1927-1993) was a Mexican American who fought for the rights of farm workers. Many farm workers faced terrible conditions, such as low pay and long workdays. Chávez worked for the common good by helping to improve these conditions.

Justice and the Rule of Law

Justice is an important democratic ideal. When people believe they have been mistreated, they can use the law to seek justice. This means that people can go to court to ask for fair treatment. The courts settle questions about the law and punish people who break the law.

Everyone in the United States must follow the laws. This is called the **rule of law**, which is another democratic ideal. It means that all people have to follow the same laws, even if they are rich and powerful. No one is above the law.

justice – fairness under the law

rule of law – the idea that everyone must obey the law

SHARE IDEAS Explain why the rule of law is important in a democracy. What would happen if some people did not have to obey the law?

◀ **People seek justice by going to court.**

KEY IDEA In the United States, our democratic ideals include equality, liberty, the common good, justice, and the rule of law.

Dr. Martin Luther King, Jr., worked hard to win voting rights for African Americans.

Changing the Law

Sometimes people believe that laws are unfair. Then people seek justice by working to change the laws.

For example, when the U.S. Constitution became law in 1789, only white men could vote in elections. Other groups of people, including African Americans, women, Asian Americans, and American Indians, were denied voting rights for many years.

In 1870, the 15th Amendment gave African American men the right to vote. But their struggle for voting rights was not over. In the South, state governments passed laws that made it very difficult for African Americans to vote.

People tried to change these unfair laws for many years. In the 1950s and 1960s, the **civil rights movement** led the federal government to pass the Voting Rights Act of 1965. This new law forced state governments to allow African Americans to vote.

civil rights movement – a social movement in the United States that worked toward equality under the law for African Americans

Other groups also worked for voting rights. Over time, constitutional amendments and other laws gave the vote to women, American Indians, Asian Americans, and citizens over the age of 18. In each case, laws were changed because people worked to change the law.

The chart below shows amendments related to voting rights. Read the quotations. How did each amendment expand the voting rights of citizens?

These amendments are examples of how people can use their rights to change the law. They show the importance of democratic ideals.

poll tax – a tax that must be paid in order to vote

Voting Rights Amendments	Year Passed
15th Amendment: *"The right of citizens of the United States to vote shall not be denied . . . on account of race, color, or previous condition of servitude."*	1870
19th Amendment: *"The right of citizens of the United States to vote shall not be denied or abridged by the United States or by any State on account of sex."*	1920
24th Amendment: *"The right of citizens of the United States to vote . . . shall not be denied . . . by reason of failure to pay any **poll tax** or other tax."*	1964
26th Amendment: *"The right of citizens of the United States, who are eighteen years of age or older, to vote shall not be denied or abridged by the United States or by any State on account of age."*	1971

KEY IDEA When laws are unfair, people work to change the laws.

SUMMARIZE

Make a chart like this one. List the five democratic ideals discussed in this chapter. Then write one way that people try to support each ideal.

Democratic Ideal	How People Support This Ideal
equality	

MAKE CONNECTIONS

There are many ways that people can work for the common good. Make a list of ways that people in your community contribute to the common good.

 STRATEGY FOCUS

Synthesize

Think about the explanation of justice on page 12. Add what you know about the struggle for voting rights. Explain how the civil rights movement supported the democratic ideal of justice.

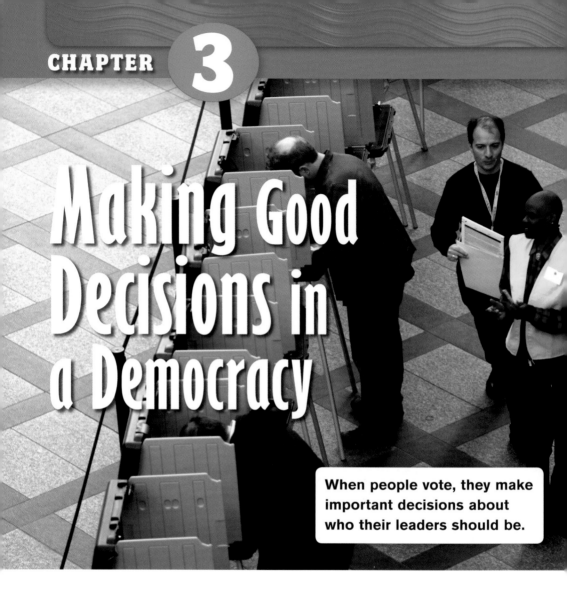

Making Good Decisions in a Democracy

When people vote, they make important decisions about who their leaders should be.

Every day you make decisions. Sometimes your decisions affect others. For example, you may decide to talk on a cell phone at a library. How does your choice affect the people around you?

Your decisions can also affect our democracy. For example, you can choose to help a political candidate get elected. You can choose to work on an **issue** that you care about.

issue – a topic of concern or importance to people

How can you make good decisions in a democracy? The first step is to be informed about possible choices. That means you need to gather information about your choices.

Learn about the issues in your community. Find out who is running for election. In a democracy, there are many ways to gather information. You can visit Web sites and watch television news programs. You can read articles that tell you more about issues and candidates.

Imagine that two people are running for public office. Before you make your choice, gather as much information as you can about each candidate. Compare the two candidates. Before you make a decision, ask yourself questions like these:

- What does each candidate think about the issues that matter to me?

- How much experience does each candidate have?

- What leadership qualities does each candidate have?

- What goals does each candidate have? How does the candidate plan to achieve those goals?

- What do other people think about this candidate?

▶ **You can become informed about a candidate or about an issue by reading news articles.**

It is also important to talk with people who have different **viewpoints**. Listen carefully. Try to understand their viewpoints. Be courteous even when you disagree.

Keep an open mind. Respect the decisions that other people make, as long as those decisions do not harm anyone. When you make decisions, think about what will be best for the common good. Thoughtful, informed decisions make a democracy stronger.

viewpoints – personal opinions or ways of thinking

It is important to hear everyone's viewpoint before making a decision.

Explore Language

Idioms

keep an open mind = be willing to consider new ideas

KEY IDEAS In a democracy, it is important to make good decisions about issues and leaders. Gather information and listen to different viewpoints before making decisions.

MAKE DECISIONS

Think about a class election. What kind of person would be a good leader for the class?

With a partner, make a list of qualities that a leader should have. Tell why you think each quality is important. List three qualities you would want to consider before making a decision.

Leadership Quality	Why It's Important
Honesty	People must be able to trust the leader.

MAKE CONNECTIONS

Think of a time when you had to make an important or difficult decision. What were your choices? What steps did you take to help you make a decision? How did you gather information to help you make your decision?

EXPAND VOCABULARY

The word **view** comes from *veoir* ("to see") in Old French. Find out about these related words. Explain how each word is related to the idea of seeing.

viewpoint   preview   review   overview

Chapter 3: Making Good Decisions in a Democracy **19**

Campaign Manager

When a person is a candate for public office, he or she needs to plan an election campaign. A candidate might hire a campaign manager to help them win votes.

A campaign manager needs strong organizing and networking skills. A campaign manager must also know how to raise money and build support among voters.

A Campaign Manager's Day

7:30 a.m.	Meet with staff. Review news articles and blogs about candidate.
11 a.m.	Attend press conference with candidate.
12:30 p.m.	Lunch with fund-raising committee.
4 p.m.	Attend radio interview with candidate.
7 p.m.	Dinner with key volunteers. Assign tasks to volunteers.
10 p.m.	Review campaign budget report.
Midnight	Check latest news headlines and poll results.

Would you like to be
a campaign manager?
Explain why or why not.

▶ **A campaign manager works hard to get a candidate elected!**

Language that Compares

When you compare, you tell how things are alike and different. The word **both** shows that two things are alike. The words **but** and **however** signal differences. You can also use **like** and **unlike** to compare two things.

EXAMPLES

Both candidates believe that the tax laws should be changed.

However, Mr. Blunt wants to raise taxes.

Unlike Mr. Blunt, Ms. Morton wants to cut taxes.

Talk About It

With a partner, reread the amendments on page 14. Compare two of the amendments. Tell how they are alike and different.

Write a Comparison

Reread the information in Chapter 2 about our democratic ideals. Choose one democratic ideal.

- Explain what life is like in a place that has this ideal.

- Describe what life would be like in a place that did not have this ideal.

- Compare life in the two places. Tell what would be the same and what would be different.

Words You Can Use	
both	like
but	unlike
however	

Look at these two political cartoons. They each have a message about voting in the United States.

- What does the large sign mean in the first cartoon?

- In the second cartoon, why do you think the woman wants to watch them count her vote?

- What is the message of each cartoon?

- Compare the two cartoons. Tell how their messages are alike and different.

22 *Our Civic Life: Democracy and Decision Making*

Key Words

Bill of Rights the part of the Constitution that lists some of our rights
The **Bill of Rights** guarantees freedom of speech.

citizen (citizens) a member of a nation
Only **citizens** can hold public office in the United States.

common good what is best for the people in a local, state, or national community
We can contribute to the **common good** by helping our neighbors.

Constitution the document that tells how the U.S. government works
The U.S. **Constitution** was written in 1787, and over the years, amendments have been added to it.

democracy (democracies) a form of government in which people elect their leaders
In a **democracy**, people have certain rights and responsibilities.

democratic ideal (democratic ideals) a belief about what is best or most important in a democracy
The common good is a **democratic ideal**.

equality when all people have the same rights under the law
Our laws help protect our **equality**.

federal government the government of the United States
The president and the Congress are parts of the **federal government**.

government (governments) a system through which some people rule others
A **government** has responsibilities to its citizens.

justice fairness under the law
We can seek **justice** in a court of law.

liberty the freedom to live the way we choose
We have **liberty** as long as we obey the law.

local government the government of a town, city, or county in a state
A **local government** often has a mayor or commissioner as its leader.

public office a position in a government
People in **public office** should act responsibly.

rule of law the idea that everyone must obey the law
The **rule of law** means that no one is above the law.

state government the government of each state in the United States
The **state government** of New York is located in Albany.

Index

MILLMARK EDUCATION CORPORATION
Ericka Markman, President and CEO; Karen Peratt, VP, Editorial Director; Lisa Bingen, VP, Marketing; Dave Willette, VP, Sales; Rachel L. Moir, VP, Operations and Production; Shelby Alinsky, Associate Editor; Ana Nuncio, Language Editor; Hanneman Productions, Photo Research; Arleen Nakama, Technology Projects

PROGRAM AUTHORS
Mary Hawley, Program Author, Instructional Design
Peggy Altoff, Program Author, Social Studies

STUDENT BOOK DEVELOPMENT Gare Thompson Associates, Inc.

BOOK DESIGN Steve Curtis Design

TECHNOLOGY Six Red Marbles

CONTENT REVIEWER
Margit McGuire, PhD, Program Director and Professor of Teacher Education, Seattle University, Seattle, WA

PROGRAM ADVISORS
Scott K. Baker, PhD, Pacific Institutes for Research, Eugene, OR
Carla C. Johnson, EdD, University of Toledo, Toledo, OH
Margit McGuire, PhD, Seattle University, Seattle, WA
Donna Ogle, EdD, National-Louis University, Chicago, IL
Betty Ansin Smallwood, PhD, Center for Applied Linguistics, Washington, DC
Gail Thompson, PhD, Claremont Graduate University, Claremont, CA
Emma Violand-Sánchez, EdD, Arlington Public Schools, Arlington, VA (retired)

PHOTO CREDITS Cover ©Todd Gipstein/CORBIS; IFC and 15b ©David Safanda/iStockphoto.com; 1a ©Lori Martin/Shutterstock; 2a and 3a ©Library of Congress; 2-3a ©Niday Picture Library/Alamy; 3b Courtesy the Lilly Library, Indiana University, Bloomington, Indiana; 4a ©Rich Koele/Shutterstock; 5b and 14a ©javarman/Shutterstock; 5c ©JustASC/Shutterstock; 6a ©AP Photo/Tina Fineberg, File; 6b ©Terrance Klassen/age fotostock; 7a ©David R. Frazier Photolibrary, Inc./Alamy; 7b ©Robert W. Ginn/Photo Edit; 7c ©Dennis MacDonald/Photo Edit; 7d ©Barrie Rokeach/Alamy; 7e ©Keith Levit/Shutterstock; 7f ©Dusan Bartolovic/Shutterstock; 8a ©Bob Daemmrich/Photo Edit; 8b ©John Neubauer/Photo Edit; 9a ©AP Photo/Evan Vucci; 9b and 9c Photos by Ken Karp; 10a ©Visions of America, LLC/Alamy; 11a ©Ted Foxx/Alamy; 11b ©AP Photo; 12a ©SuperStock/agefotostock; 13a ©Bettmann/CORBIS; 15a ©Jeff Greenberg/Photo Edit; 16a ©AP Photo/David Zalubowski; 17a ©David Young-Wolff/Photo Edit; 18a ©Kayte Deioma/Photo Edit; 20a ©Stephanie Kuykendal/Corbis; 22a ©2008 Jeff Parker, Florida Today, and PoliticalCartoons.com; 22b Jeff Stahler: ©Columbus Dispatch/Dist. by Newspaper Enterprise Association, Inc.; 24a ©Glen Jones/Shutterstock

Copyright ©2009 Millmark Education Corporation

All rights reserved. Reproduction of the whole or any part of the contents without written permission from the publisher is prohibited. Millmark Education and ConceptLinks are registered trademarks of Millmark Education Corporation.

Published by Millmark Education Corporation
PO Box 30239
Bethesda, MD 20824

ISBN-13: 978-1-4334-0693-5

Printed in the USA

10 9 8 7 6 5 4 3 2 1